You Are

The Cyan Ocean

HIGHLINE HOUSE

YOU ARE THE CYAN OCEAN.

Copyright ©2023 by Kate Manser and Kelly Trueman.

All rights reserved.

No part of this book shall be reused or reproduced

without express written permission.

Published by Highline House Publishing.

Writing and interior design by Kate Manser.

Cover and illustrations by Kelly Trueman.

Paperback ISBN: 978-1-952018-06-0

Hardcover ISBN: 978-1-952018-07-7

eBook ISBN: 978-1-952018-08-4

We're all souls
swimming together
in the great sea of life.
Just keep swimming.

For Cyan, Weston, and Lane

You are the cyan ocean

and the gray stormy sea.

The kind deed

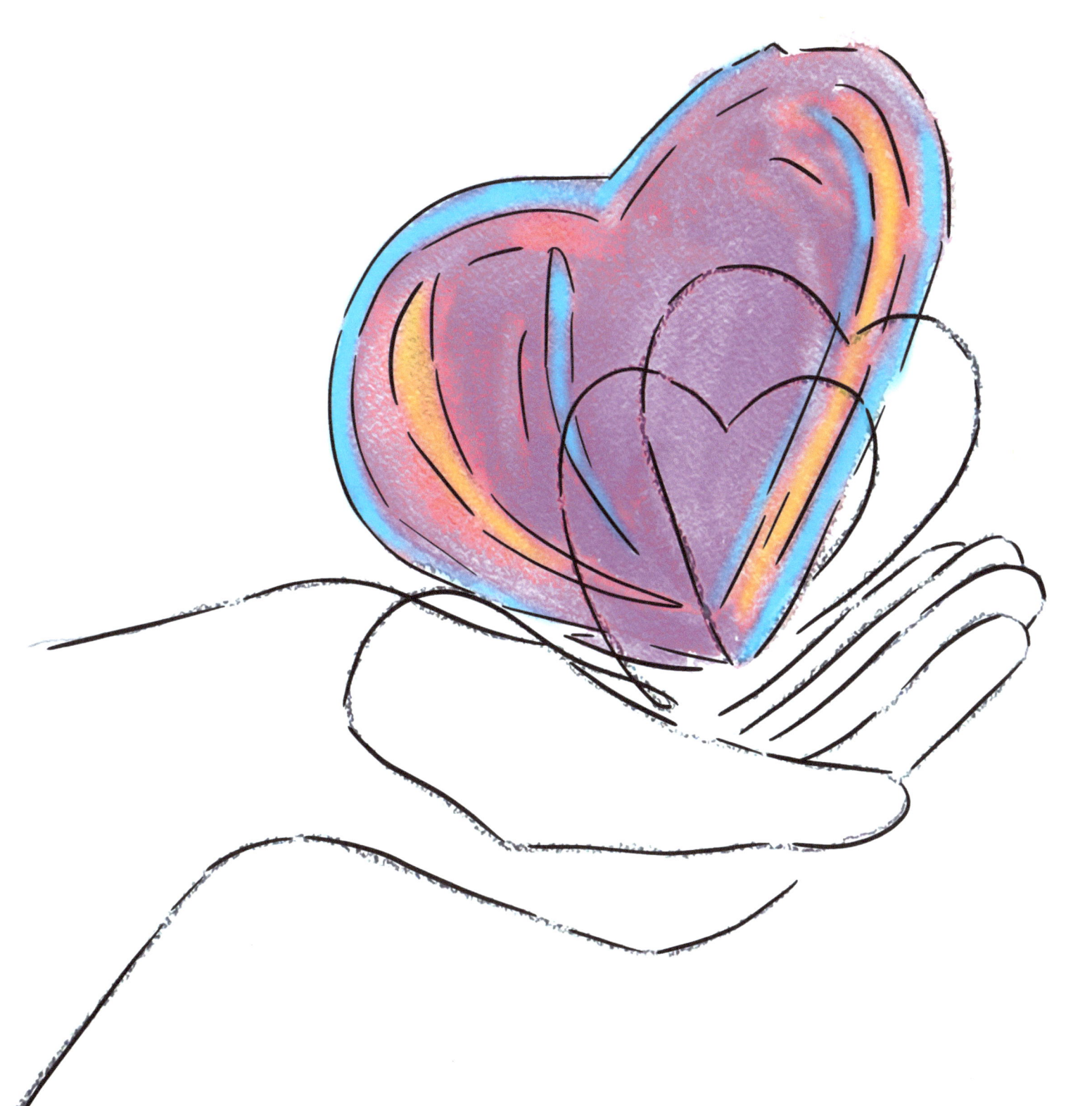

and everything in
b e t w e e n.

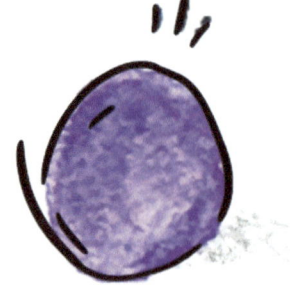

You are the tiniest of the tiny ...

And the biggest of the big!

You are the seahorse in the reef

and the giraffe

munching a leaf.

You are the surfer

and you are the wave.

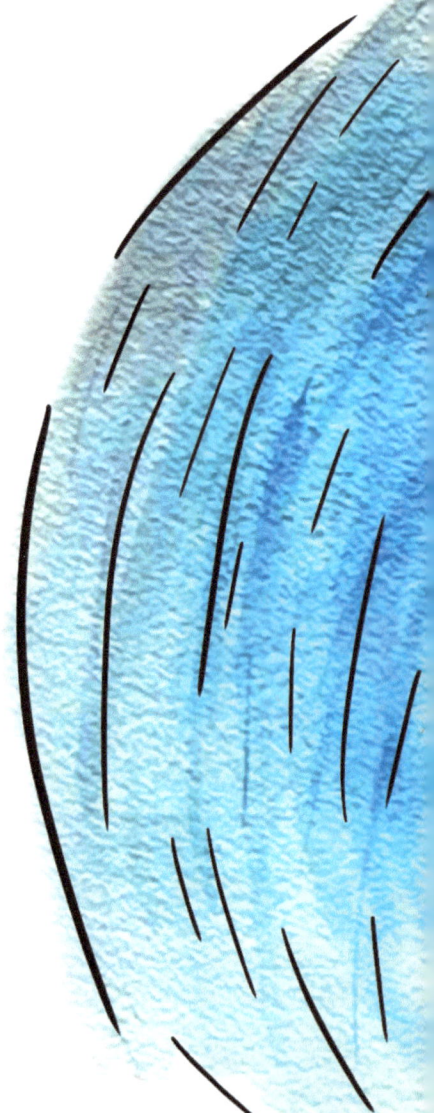

You are the moon,
the stars,
the astronaut

and even the rocket!

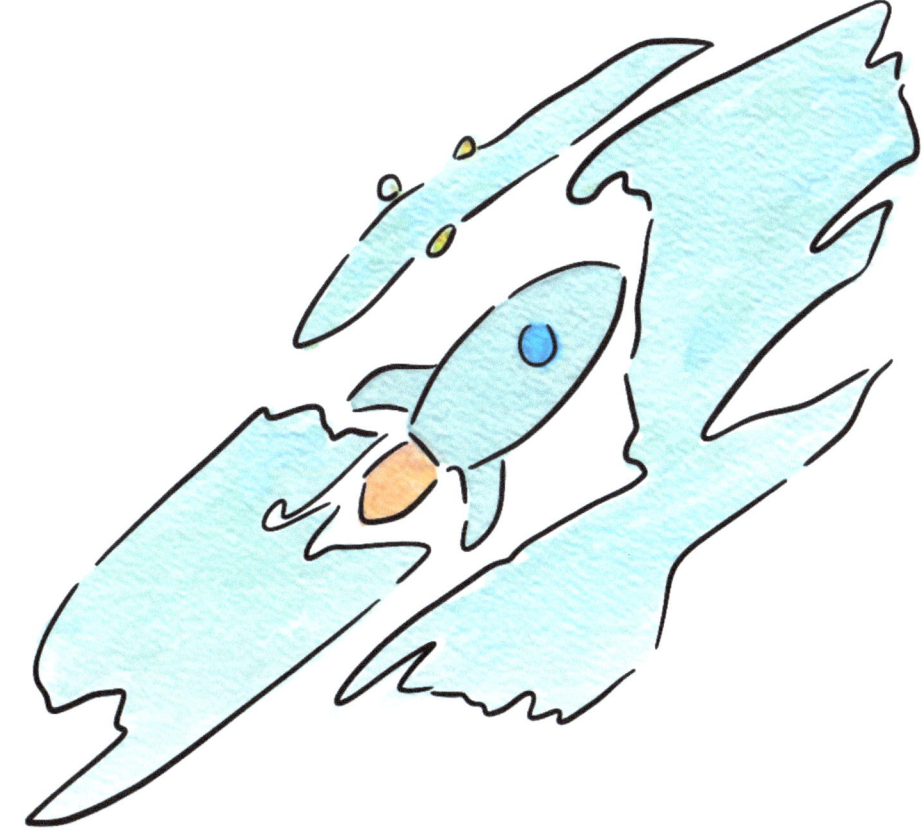

Some days, you'll be the one who gets picked first...

other days, you'll be the one who hustles out last.

You are every tiny bug

and every great tree.

You're every delicate flower
(and the spiky ones, too!)

You are the honey

the bee

You are the smile,
and you are the sea.

You are all the love,

all the hope,

and all the peace.

We are all together

We are all connected

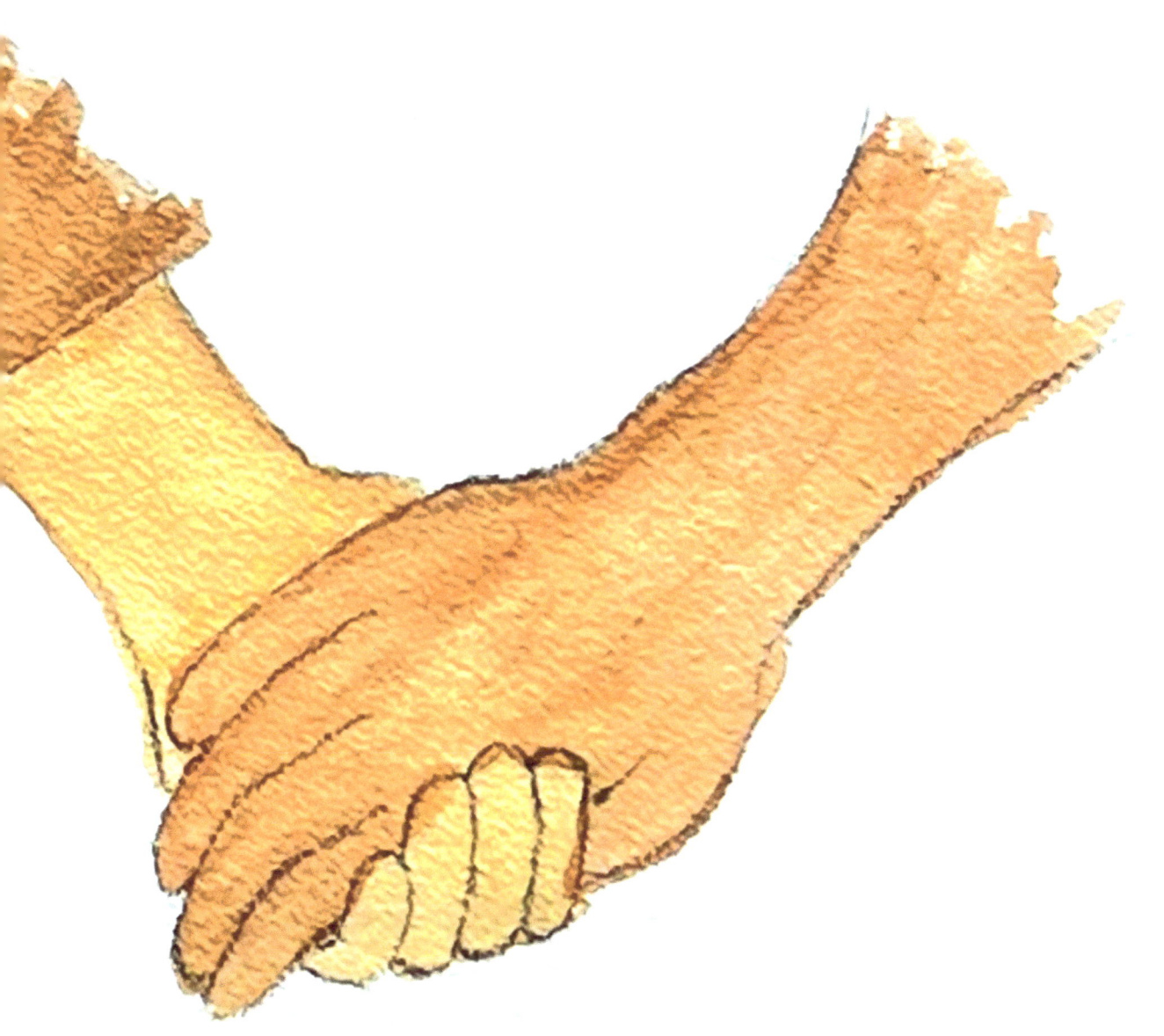

Conversation Starters for Adults & Kids

Deepen the experience with conversations about consciousness, loneliness, bullying, and world peace.

- What do all humans have in common?
- Do you think all living beings have feelings, including plants and animals?
- Tell me about a time you saw someone get left out or bullied. What can you do when you see that happen in the future?
- Tell me about the last time you felt lonely.
    - What made you feel that way? What did you do to feel better?
- Draw a picture that shows all humans around the world coexisting in peace.

About the Author

@thealivekate

Kate Manser helps humankind feel more alive. She is a visionary creator and spiritual teacher whose works include speaking, books, large-scale sculpture, and aliveness experiences. Kate loves adventure, the color neon yellow-green, olive oil & honey on vanilla ice cream, and quiet moments of peace and wonder.

About the Illustrator

Kelly Trueman is a wife, mother, and teacher. She holds a Masters degree in Early and Elementary Education. She is married to her high school sweetheart and they are raising their two beautiful boys. She loves spending time with her family: hiking, camping, and playing together as well as finding creative and beautiful opportunities to experience life.

A word from the authors

Dear reader,

Thank you for taking a chance on our book. We wrote it with love and a vision for world peace. We hope it has touched your heart and uplifted your spirit.

Your voice truly matters. It would mean the world to us if you would take a moment to write a heartfelt review for this book on Goodreads, Amazon, or wherever you purchased it. Your kind feedback is so appreciated and helps get this book into the hands of other children and adults whom it may help.

With all our love,
Kate and Kelly

Printed in the USA
CPSIA information can be obtained
at www.ICGtesting.com
LVHW061110171223
766490LV00049B/1044